colors

W9-AIB-753

**Photography
George Siede and Donna Preis**

Louis Weber, C.E.O.
Publications International, Ltd.
7373 North Cicero Avenue
Lincolnwood, Illinois 60646

ISBN 0–7853–1282–X

Publications International, Ltd.

red

wagon

strawberries

hat

shirt

ball

overalls

tulip

shoes

orange

jack-o-lantern

carrots

flowers

oranges

yellow

bananas

lemon

ducks

raincoat

umbrella

galoshes

blue

sunglasses

dice

blueberries

jeans

green

frog

green beans

lettuce

apples

purple

teddy bear

flower

gumballs

bubble

brown

puppy

cookies

peanuts

pancake

black

kitten

mouse

penguin

hat

white

bunny

milk

snowball

ghost